Your Next Steps

What To Do When Your
Spouse Is Unfaithful

Jill Savage

Copyright 2017 Jill Savage
Revised Edition 2021

All rights reserved. No part of this book may be reproduced in any form without permission in writing from the author, except in the case of brief quotations embodied in critical articles or review.

All scripture quotations, unless otherwise indicated, are taken from the *Holy Bible, New International Version*, NIV. Copyright 2011 by Biblica, Inc.

Scripture quotations marked ESV are taken from *The Holy Bible, English Standard Version.* Copyright 2001 by Crossway Bibles.

All websites listed in the book are accurate at the time of publication, but may change in the future or cease to exist. Groups and organizations are listed for informational purposes, and does not imply author endorsement of their activities.

Table of Contents

Introduction	*5*
Step #1: Connect with the Friend Who Understands	*9*
Step #2: Drop Your Anchor in His Word	*13*
Step #3: Be Still	*16*
Step #4: Fight on your Knees	*18*
Step #5: Take Care of You	*21*
Step #6: Accept Help	*23*
Step #7: Understand This Isn't About You	*26*
Step #8: Own What's Yours	*29*
Step #9: Set Boundaries	*33*
Step #10: Choose Love	*36*
Final Thoughts	*40*
Appendix A: Mark and Jill Savage Resources	*44*
Appendix B: Bible Verses for Hard Times	*46*
Appendix C: Recommended Reading and Resources	*50*

Introduction

"I'm leaving. I have no intention of returning. I'm pursuing the other relationship and I want a divorce."

With those words, my husband walked out of the house and my life turned upside down.

I had never pictured myself a single parent. I had never imagined my marriage would experience such a painful breach of trust. I had never experienced such horrific pain and rejection.

You've picked up this book because you're where I was. The world is dark. The grief is real. Your heart is ripped to pieces and you're not sure you're ever going to experience joy again.

I understand.

You feel alone in a world that seems to be moving forward while you feel left behind. You're suddenly eating alone. Sitting at church alone. Taking care of the kids alone. You've likely never felt as alone as you do right now.

Maybe you're not physically alone, but you're emotionally alone. Your spouse hasn't left, but he or she isn't committed either. You've discovered there's someone else. You're not sure what to do and you seem to be the only one willing to do something.

Or maybe you're both willing to make it work, but it seems too big, too overwhelming, and too painful to even feel hopeful. You wonder if your marriage really can make it.

One morning about two weeks after my husband left, I found myself curled up in bed crying my eyes out and begging God to relieve the pain. I'd sent my two brokenhearted teenagers off to school (our three older kids, who were young adults out on their own, were also emotionally wrecked at their father's choices) and had crawled back in bed. I just wanted to sleep so I wouldn't feel the pain.

I'd discovered the affair seven months earlier. He'd recommitted to us, then started communicating with her again, then recommitted to our marriage, then back to her….back and forth six times. Then one day he left and indicated he really was done. I've never felt such emotional pain as I did in the two weeks after he left.

So this particular morning I awoke with swollen eyes as I had every day for the two weeks before. I went through the motions to get my boys off to school and then I did my best to make the reality of my world go away by attempting to sleep, begging God to change my circumstances.

In that dark moment, God took me back a few years earlier to a Hearts at Home conference for moms where I had heard author and speaker, Jennifer Rothschild, speak about losing her sight at the age of 17. As she shared her story, she made this simple statement: *It is not well with my circumstances, but it is well with my soul.* I remembered her saying it but it really didn't apply to my life at the time. On this dark February morning, however, it most definitely applied to me. It most definitely was NOT well with my circumstances. Was it even possible that it could be well with my soul?

That was the day I turned a corner in my grief. That was the day I began to pick up the pieces. That was the day I saw just a glimmer of the possibility of peace, hope, and joy someday again in the future.

I crawled out of bed and found my Bible. It was not well with my circumstances but I was determined that it would be well with my soul and I knew I had to begin that journey with God.

That day was over eight years ago. My marriage made it, but even if it hadn't, I want you to know that I would be okay today. And regardless of what happens in your world, I want you to know that you will be okay, too.

What do we need to do for it to be well with our soul? I want to share with you ten steps that will get you headed in the right direction. They're not easy, but they're important for keeping your head and your heart in the right place even in the midst of difficult circumstances.

Step #1

Connect with the Friend Who Understands

I don't know where you are in your faith journey, but now is the time to dig deep spiritually. You can't do this on your own. You need God's strength, hope, and wisdom in the middle of your mess. Don't worry, you don't need to clean yourself up before you come to God. The Bible says that God is the potter and we are the clay. Have you ever seen a potter's hands when he's molding a clay pot? They're dirty. Very, very dirty. So we can be sure that God's not afraid to get His hands dirty.

I'm going to give you the short and to-the-point version of what it means to have a personal relationship with God. We're not talking religion—we're talking relationship. A living, breathing, day by day, moment by moment, He-never-leaves-your-side relationship with the God of the universe. Bottom line: God created us to have relationship with Him. Adam and Eve's choices in the Garden of Eden broke that relationship with God. After that, relationship with a Holy God and an unholy people was built around sacrifices. Only the High Priest could be the connection between the people and God. Then God sent His Son, Jesus, to be the Ultimate Sacrifice, the final High Priest who loved us so much He died a horrendous death on the cross for us. Three days later he rose from the dead and is now our advocate in heaven.

Jesus has His hand extended to you…will you take it? Will you admit that you can't do life on your own? Will you allow God to take His place in the driver's seat of your life?

Here's the most incredible part of walking through your difficult circumstances with Jesus: He gets it. Seriously, He does. Yet, here's how Jesus is your Friend who understands:

He was betrayed. Jesus had 12 close friends. The Bible calls them the disciples. These were His buddies. They ate together. Traveled together. Loved on people together. They did life together! One of His friends, Judas, decided that the temptation of 30 pieces of silver was worth chasing. He betrayed Jesus and told His enemies where to find Him, ultimately resulting in His death on the cross.

He was disappointed. When Jesus knew that a horrendous death was around the corner, He went with His friends to a place called the Garden of Gethsemane. The Bible tells us He was so overwhelmed with what awaited Him, He was sweating blood. He asked His friends to pray with Him and they agreed to. So Jesus told them to stay and watch and pray near the entrance to the garden while Jesus went off to pour out His heart to His Father in heaven. When He returned from praying alone, He found His friends asleep. Can you imagine His disappointment? His friends let Him down!

He cried. When Jesus's friend Lazarus died, Jesus cried. He let His emotions go and allowed His grief to be expressed. He knows the pain of loss.

He was tired. The Bible tells several stories about Jesus being tired from His journeys (remember, they had to walk everywhere back then!). One particular story in the Bible says that after teaching on a mountainside, Jesus crawled in a boat and fell fast asleep. He was absolutely exhausted.

He was tempted. Jesus fasted for 40 days and during that time the enemy tempted Him in many different ways. Jesus responded to each temptation with God's Word. He stood strong during a time when it would have been easy to give in.

The Bible tells us that God draws close to the brokenhearted. You are brokenhearted, so God is near. My prayer for you is that, as you let Him lead you through this time, you will feel His presence.

If you've never accepted Jesus as your Savior and you're not quite sure how to pray, here's a heartfelt prayer that will get your started:

"God, my life is a mess. My heart is broken. My pain is excruciating. I can't do this on my own. I need you. Please forgive me for trying to do things my way. Please forgive me for living life without you. Thank you for going to the cross for me. Thank you for loving me. Thank you for not leaving me. I'm going to move aside and let you lead from this day forward. In Jesus Name...Amen."

There's nothing fancy about talking to God. No right or wrong words. Just talk to Him like you would a friend sitting in front of you. He truly is a Friend who understands.

Truth for Today

"Now that we know what we have—Jesus, this great High Priest with ready access to God—let's not let it slip through our fingers.

We don't have a priest who is out of touch with our reality. He's been through weakness and testing, experienced it all—all but the sin. So let's walk right up to him and get what he is so ready to give. Take the mercy, accept the help."
Hebrews 4:14-16, The Message

Lord, I'm weary. I'm scared. My heart is broken. I know you've been there too and I'm so glad you really are a Friend who understands. Help me to keep bringing all that I'm fearing and feeling to you. In Jesus Name. Amen.

Step #2
Drop Your Anchor in His Word

Through my tears, I dug in the living room for my Bible. It had been weeks since I'd opened it. I carried it to my bedroom because I was determined that it would be the last thing I would see before I went to sleep and the first thing I'd reach for in the morning. I usually only had the energy to read a few verses at night and a few in the morning before my kids needed me. And while I slept, my Bible was carefully placed on my husband's empty pillow.

Your world has been turned upside down. Your life doesn't look anything like it did before. It's disorienting and feels unsteady. It probably feels like you're a ship being tossed about in a storm. You've lost your way and you have to find your True North again. You need an anchor to keep you from drifting off course.

God's way of handling things is different than the world's way of handing things. You'll be tempted to lash out and throw your hurt back at your spouse. But God wants you to respond with restraint. He wants you to express your pain without throwing your pain at the one who hurt you.

In order to do that, you'll need your marching orders. Read

Philippians, Romans, Colossians, and 1st and 2nd Corinthians. If you want to know Jesus better, read Matthew, Mark, Luke, or John. Highlight or underline verses that mean something to you (yes, you can write in your Bible!). If something really touches you, make it the screensaver on your computer or phone, or write it on an index card and put it on your refrigerator or bathroom mirror.

God will use His Word to speak to you. He will give you valuable perspective and tell you what to do. When the waves of uncertainty toss you back and forth, God's Word will anchor and steady you.

God will also speak to you through the Holy Spirit, prompting you to do things in ways that only make sense to God.

Here are some important verses for you during this dark time. (You'll find more in Appendix A!)

Psalm 46:1-3 God is our refuge and strength, an ever-present help in trouble. Therefore we will not fear, though the earth give way and the mountains fall into the heart of the sea, though its waters roar and foam and the mountains quake with their surging.

Proverbs 18:10 The name of the Lord is a strong tower; the righteous run into it and are safe.

Nehemiah 8:10 Do not grieve, for the joy of the Lord is your strength.

Isaiah 41:10 So do not fear, for I am with you; do not be dismayed, for I am your God. I will strengthen you and help you; I will uphold you with my righteous right hand.

Isaiah 26: 3-4 Those of steadfast mind you keep in peace—because they trust in you. Trust in the Lord forever, for in the Lord God you have an everlasting rock.

1 Chronicles 16:11 Seek the LORD and his strength; seek his presence continually.

Truth for Today

"Therefore, we who have fled to him for refuge can have great confidence as we hold to the hope that lies before us. This hope is a strong and trustworthy anchor for our souls."
Hebrews 18b-19a, NLT

Lord, I'm feeling tossed around by my circumstances and my emotions. I need you to be my anchor. My true north. I need you to give me my marching orders. Show me how to respond to what is happening in your way that is different than I feel like responding. In Jesus Name. Amen

Step #3

Be Still

I sat in the counselor's office, eyes so swollen from an hour of crying they were barely slits in my face. "Jill, I have a homework assignment for you," he said. "Ok," I responded, willing to do anything to get my life and my marriage put back together. "I want you to sit for 20 minutes a day." "And do what?" I asked. "Be still," he said. Focus on just breathing in and breathing out."

Exasperated, I said, "That seems like a waste of 20 minutes. I'm a git-it-done girl." "I know," he responded. "It's time for you to be a 'Quiet-your-soul' kind of girl." This kind of assignment messed with my Type A driven personality. But I listened and decided to give it a try for the week between my appointments.

Day one, I barely made it five minutes. I squirmed, assembled my grocery list in my head, and watched the clock. "This is not for me," I declared under my breath. But I had committed to do it for the week so I tried again on day two. This time I made it ten minutes. I focused on my breathing and found myself actually relaxing just a little bit. Day three I again focused on my breathing and somewhere between ten and fifteen minutes I FELL

ASLEEP. Sitting in my recliner. In the middle of the day. This girl, who can't sleep unless she's laying down in a dark room, slept. I woke up about twenty minutes later with the most incredible sense of peace. The Bible describes this as a "peace that passes all understanding."

My chaotic circumstances were creating a chaotic soul. That day I experienced the reality of "it is not well with my circumstances, but it is well with my soul." Deep in my soul I knew that whether my husband returned or not, I would be okay. I knew that God was with me. I knew that my God would never leave me.

You will be tempted to control. You'll be tempted to grasp at every straw you see. You'll be tempted to do, do, and do some more to change your reality. I want to encourage you to BE STILL. Be a seeker of internal peace. This is where God stills your soul, clears your head, and gives you the peace you're looking for.

Truth for Today

"Be still and know that I am God."
Psalm 46:10

Lord, I feel the need to do something! Help me to still my body and soul and simply be with you. Calm the chaos in my soul so I can experience the peace I know only comes from you. In Jesus Name. Amen.

Step #4

Fight on your Knees

When a marriage falls apart, there's often conflict. Disagreements increase and the temptation to argue and fight with words is very real. Yet doing so will be fighting the wrong fight.

Spiritual warfare is very real. There is an enemy that does not want your marriage to make it. This enemy comes to steal, kill, and destroy. He wants to do that to us individually and in our relationships. So the first place you need to fight spiritual warfare is inside your head and your heart. Do not let the enemy steal your peace. That's why Steps 1, 2, and 3 are so very important. Confess your ugly thoughts. Ask for forgiveness for where you fall short. Pray for wisdom for your daily marching orders.

Somewhere around three weeks after my husband left, a dear friend spoke some powerful words to me, "Jill," she said, "you have to be careful not to make saving your marriage an idol." Wow! She just about knocked me over with those words. Why? Because I *was* making saving my marriage an idol. An idol is anything we give more time and energy to than God. I was so focused on saving my marriage that I'd moved God to second place. I had to confess that and ask God for forgiveness, putting Him back on the throne of my heart.

If your spouse is having an affair, pray a hedge of thorns around him or her. Pray a hedge of thorns around the "other" person. This is a way to pray for conflict to happen between the two of them. Doing so can open an unfaithful spouse's eyes that this new relationship isn't that much different than their marriage. It reminds them that the grass isn't really greener on the other side of the fence.

Pray powerfully. When fear creeps in, speak the name of Jesus. Ask God for what you need. Pray for your spouse's relationship with God. Pray against distraction. Pray for wisdom, patience, and the ability to respond rather than react to any interaction with your spouse. Pray as you drive, as you walk, as you get ready in the morning. Pray throughout your day. You don't have to stop and fold your hands and bow your head to pray. Just talk to God throughout the day as you would a friend who is right beside you.

In order to move forward emotionally and spiritually, you'll have to forgive. This is part of your fight on your knees. Unforgiveness keeps our heart cluttered and unavailable to God. It keeps us bound up. Forgiveness frees us to move forward and to be able to respond to God. Forgiveness also isn't "once and done." You'll need to forgive each time an offense comes to mind. That may be dozens of times a day, especially in the early days, weeks, and months.

Don't confuse forgiveness with trust. Forgiveness is a choice you must make to experience peace. Trust is earned over time, if and when both of you are working to rebuild your relationship.

As you pray, make sure you also express your gratefulness for what you still have. Thank God for a good night of sleep, or an honest conversation with your kids, or the support of extended family, or the provision of a job you have or what your spouse is still providing. Gratitude helps us find balance in the midst of a dark season.

Truth for Today

"Pray without ceasing."
I Thessalonians 5:17, ESV

Lord, help me to fight this battle on my knees. When I'm tempted to fight with my spouse who is lost, help me to respond in a way that disarms them. Remind me that I am never alone and that I can talk to you every minute of the day. Help me to listen and trust that you are talking to me too. In Jesus Name. Amen.

Step #5
Take Care of You

I'd heard people share about difficult emotional situations where they absolutely lost their appetite and just couldn't even make themselves eat. I had never understood that. I tend to like food and I'm usually not one to miss a meal.

The first few days after my husband left, however, I absolutely couldn't even make myself eat. It was as if my digestive system completely shut down. I lost nearly 10 pounds in a week. That's not healthy at all.

Eventually I had to force myself to take in nutrition, stay hydrated, and even take a daily walk. I didn't feel like doing any of those, but knew I had to start taking care of myself in order to have the energy to return to work and be the mom I needed to be. My five children were hurting as much as I was and I needed to help them sort through their emotions even as I was sorting through mine.

You'll be tempted not to eat. You'll forget to drink water. Exercise will be the last thing on your radar during these disorienting circumstances. Yet you must put self-care at the top of your priority list. Not only will it give you the physical energy you need, but it will also help your mental health. A walk helps you get out of the house and reminds you the world is bigger than your difficult situation.

When you board an airplane and they always give the emergency instructions before takeoff. No matter what airline you fly, you'll hear the instruction that if you're traveling with someone who needs assistance, put on your own oxygen mask first before assisting others. What they know and understand is that you're unable to help others if you don't help yourself first. The same principle applies here. You have to put on your own oxygen mask first in order to stay functioning in your everyday world even in the midst of these difficult circumstances.

Truth for Today

"I can do all things through Christ who strengthens me."
Philippians 4:13, NKJV

Lord, I want to crawl in a ball and pretend that none of this is happening, but I know I can't. I need to continue to function. I need to take care of the body and soul you have given me. When I'm all out of energy, let me allow you to fill my gaps. I can do what I need to do today with your help. In Jesus Name. Amen.

Step #6
Accept Help

For many of us, we equate asking for help or accepting help with failure. If that's you, it's time to put that lie to rest. It's not a sign of failure if you ask for help...it's actually a sign of strength. You can't do this on your own. You may need to ask for carpooling help from a friend or neighbor. You may need to ask for emotional help from a counselor. You may even need to ask for financial help from your church or a local food pantry. Now is the time to set pride aside and get the help you need.

When Mark was gone, I had a friend who called me each time she went to the grocery store, asking if I needed anything. Her offer of help kept me out of public settings where an innocent interaction with an acquaintance I might see while shopping would easily result in tears when they innocently asked, "Hi Jill! How are you?" I was grateful for her offer and almost always had her pick up something for me.

I also called my boys' school counselor, asking her to notify the teachers of the emotional earthquake they were experiencing in their life. Was I embarrassed to make that call? Yes, absolutely.

But was it important? Most definitely.

Sometimes the help you need to ask for is wisdom. You'll find yourself in all kinds of unknown and unexpected situations. Ask others to help you think through what you should do, but ALWAYS balance it with what you sense the Holy Spirit is leading you to do. Here's an example of a time I had to do that. Some dear friends of ours were getting married in Mexico several weeks after Mark left. We had airfare tickets and our hotel accommodations settled months earlier. Should I go or should I not? Every friend and family member counseled me not to go, but when I prayed I felt like God was telling me to go. What a difficult decision! Finally, I decided to follow the leading of the Holy Spirit. I'm glad I went because we had some important and healing conversations that week in Mexico. We didn't come home all healed, but there were baby steps made that week.

If you don't have a strong family or friendship circle, you may feel isolated. You may need to pick up the phone and reach out. When you do that, you may not get a positive response from everyone you reach out to, but don't let that stop you. Make your needs known to others. If they offer to help, say yes and thank them! Someday you'll be in a place where you have the time, energy, and resources to be on the "giving help" side again. For now, flex your receiving muscles, asking for help and accepting any help offered.

Truth for Today

"Two are better than one… If either of them falls down, one can help the other up."
Ecclesiastes 4:9-10a, NIV

Lord, I fear being a burden to others, but I know I need help. Give me the courage and the strength to both ask for help and accept help. Deepen my understanding that when others help me, they are blessed in the giving. You lived life in community with others. Help me to do the same during this hard season of my life. In Jesus Name. Amen.

Step #7

Understand This Isn't About You

As much as it feels like rejection, the truth is your spouse's decisions are far more about his/her own disillusionment and confusion than it is about you. I know it FEELS like he or she is rejecting you. I also know it's possible they are SAYING they were unfaithful or they are leaving because of you, but don't take that bait!

Don't get me wrong, I'm not suggesting that you haven't contributed to your broken relationship in some way (we'll talk about that in Step #8). I'm just saying that it's important that you see your spouse through the lens of being lost and confused. Resist making too much of this about you. Why? Because you'll spend your time and energy chasing the wrong thing.

You'll be chasing your spouse's acceptance of you instead of pursuing integrity. You'll be making "saving your marriage" an idol instead of worshipping the One who will never leave you. You'll be keeping your eyes on the mountains instead of looking at the Mountain Mover.

When you see your spouse as lost and confused (or emotionally constipated as I said to a dear friend dealing with her husband's affair and lack of concern over what it was doing to his kids), you'll begin to see him or her with compassion. When you have compassion for someone, it increases your patience, your kindness, and your love for them. You need this in order to respond to him or her in a Christ-like way rather than throwing your pain back at them.

When I discovered the affair, the pain of betrayal was tangible. My heart actually hurt. I would bet you're feeling that way, too. I saw my husband as a liar, a deceiver, a man who broke his vows. I dug out every card he'd given me over our then 28 years of marriage, ripping them up and throwing them in the trash. The despair was real and I was only looking at him through the lens of MY pain.

However, when I was able to look at him through the lens of HIS pain, my feelings changed. I saw him as confused, lost, struggling, disillusioned, trying to fill the God-shaped hole in his heart with everything but God. I began to realize that this wasn't really about me at all. Yes, there were things I needed to look at in my own life. However, the pain my husband caused me was really an outpouring of the pain in his own heart. This increased my compassion, caused me to pray intensely for him, and helped me to see him the way God sees him.

Yes, your spouse betrayed you. The pain is very real. However, the pain deep in your spouse's heart is very real, too. He or she may cover it up with accusations, blame, anger, and even arrogance, but deep inside is pain that has probably been there since childhood. That pain is likely unknown to your loved one, but it's there. Remembering that will help you see your spouse through eyes of grace, love, and even forgiveness.

Truth for Today

"Therefore, as God's chosen people, holy and dearly loved, clothe yourselves with compassion, kindness, humility, gentleness, and patience."
Colossians 3:12, NIV

Lord, help me to see my spouse through your eyes of compassion. Help me to recognize that he/she is making poor choices in response to his/her own pain. Instill in me kindness, compassion, humility, gentleness, and patience at a time when I feel anything but those things. In Jesus Name. Amen.

Step #8
Own What's Yours

It's true that it takes two people to marry but only one to divorce. However, unhealthy relational habits in marriage are contributed to from both sides. While you don't want to take your spouse's affair, decision to leave, or distance in the relationship personally, you do need to own what's yours.

Now is the time to do a relationship audit. What's your junk in the trunk? What do you bring to the table that's caused damage in your marriage? Have you put your extended family before your spouse? Been controlling? Always had to have the last word? Have you tried harder to change your spouse than accept him/her? Have you been passive in the relationship? Have you been unwilling to step into your spouse's world and do something he or she has longed to do together? Have you let your fears get in the way of living life? Have you emasculated your man by mothering him? Have you been unloving to your wife, only showing her physical touch when you want sex? Have you been disrespectful in your tone of voice? Have you let your past (from childhood or a previous relationship) affect your present?

Now's the time to get honest with yourself. When I did this, I had to come face to face with my tendency to avoid emotion. I grew up in a family that was strong through hard times. We "bucked up" and pushed through difficult things. I cried in private, didn't let other people's criticism affect me, and prioritized facts over feelings. What I didn't understand is that my strong outer veneer was sending a message to my husband that I didn't need him. Quite frankly, I believed I didn't need anybody. I was independent and strong and I thought that was good. It can be in the business world, but it doesn't serve you very well in relationships.

I also had to look at the way I treated my husband. When I got honest with myself, I had to admit that much of the time I "parented" him. That's not healthy in a marriage at all. In fact, I had to be honest that I was emasculating him when I did that.

SPECIAL NOTE TO THE LADIES READING THIS: If you're a strong woman married to a passive man who has left or found someone else, I strongly suggest that you order the book The God-Empowered Wife *by Karen Haught. Karen really understands this "superior wife" syndrome and how to turn it around. Her book was an absolute game-changer for me and really helped me see the damage I was doing to my husband. It helped me own my stuff and turn my actions around.*

When we own our stuff, it's important we feel conviction but stay away from condemnation. Conviction says "I did a bad thing," but condemnation says, "I did a bad thing so I'm a bad person." Conviction is from God and condemnation is from the enemy. We want conviction because that's when our conscience is pricked and it brings about repentance—or a 180-degree change in direction. Conviction allows us to apologize and ask for forgiveness for the unhealthy habits we bring to our marriage. Condemnation tells us we're getting what we deserve and keeps us in a hopeless place that says, "it doesn't matter anyway."

If you begin to identify things you need to own, first do business with God. Confess your junk and ask for forgiveness. The minute you ask, God will grant you forgiveness and wipe the slate clean! Then it's time to do business with your spouse. If you can communicate what you're learning in person, then do. Apologize and ask for forgiveness. If you're unable to have conversation, consider writing a letter. It's entirely possible and even probable that your spouse will feel like you're saying whatever you need to say to get them back. Or that he or she will say it's "a little too late" for that. Communicate that you understand why they might feel that way, but reassure them that the learning curve is real and you're working to make the changes you need to make.

Remember, you need to get rid of your junk in the trunk regardless of whether your marriage makes it or not. When you're keeping God on the throne of your heart, He's cleaning you up from the inside out. This is far more about your Audience of One (God) than your marriage. The more you become like Christ, the better it is for your life and your marriage.

This is where a counselor or coach can be helpful for digging deep and sorting through your stuff. This may be a place where you need to ask for help (and if finances are challenging, many counselors offer sliding scales based upon income). Whatever it takes, work to own your own stuff. It will give you understanding and freedom in a powerful, healing way.

Truth for Today

"You can't whitewash your sins and get by with it; you find mercy by admitting and leaving them."
Proverbs 28:13, The Message

Lord, I know that I didn't cause my spouse to be unfaithful, but I have contributed to the dysfunction in our marriage. Help me to see what I've brought to the table. Help me to identify the places I need to grow. Bring conviction in my heart so I can own what I need to own. And thank you for your forgiveness in it all. In Jesus Name. Amen.

Step #9
Set Boundaries

I sat in the counselor's office absolutely exhausted from a sleepless night. I had come home late from a speaking engagement and found my husband asleep in bed holding his phone. As I carefully removed the phone, I glanced at the screen and upon reading the conversation, I wanted to throw up. He was chatting with a woman and they were talking about their time at a hotel earlier that week. I actually went downstairs and called her on my husband's phone. I told her I knew and that she needed to be a woman of integrity and break off the relationship before it broke up a family. I cried all night and never went to bed. We had a counseling appointment scheduled for the next morning so I decided I would confront him there.

When I brought it up in the counselor's office, my husband confirmed what I'd seen and stated that he had no desire to leave the other relationship. Eventually the counselor separated us and spoke to us each individually. I asked him what I should do. He said, "Jill, if he agrees to get help (at that time the counselor was recommending help for sexual addiction), then he can stay at your house. If, however, he refuses to get help, you need to ask him to leave." That was my first education in boundaries.

That day my husband did agree to get help and I didn't ask him to leave. However, he eventually left and that's when I began to set boundaries. What I learned is that boundaries are tough love and they are important for protecting your heart (and your children's hearts if you have kids), but they are also valuable for the offending spouse to feel the consequences of their own choices.

One boundary I immediately put in place was that he couldn't come home to get his personal items. He could tell me what he wanted and I would arrange a pick-up location for him to get his things. This is where I had to ask for help. I asked two friends to come over and pack up his clothing and requested items. I just couldn't bring myself to do it. It was too painful. One of them offered to be the pick-up point for him so he had to make arrangements with her and her husband to get his things.

Another boundary was changing the locks on the house. He had left and couldn't enter the house anytime he pleased. It was too painful for our boys for him to just "show up." With the coaching of my counselor, I set up off-site connecting points for the boys and their dad. This kept our home an emotionally safe place for our boys (I also established our home as a "cry zone" for my two teenage boys. I wanted them to feel safe to express whatever they were feeling. No more "buck up" messages for us!).

Don't feel guilty about boundaries. I recently was encouraging a young mom walking through her husband's infidelity and separation. She has two small children and is expecting their third child in a few months. She hated to deny her husband the opportunity to be at their child's birth but she didn't want him to be there either because he was now living with his mistress. She said, "I don't want him to be there but I don't know if I can live with myself knowing I took that experience away from him." I told her, "You didn't take it away from him; he took it away from himself." Resist the temptation to "own" a consequence that isn't yours to own. That, in and of itself, is an important boundary to set in your heart.

Truth for Today

"A man reaps what he sows."
Galatians 6:7b

Lord, help me to draw lines where lines need to be drawn. I don't want to steal the struggle from my spouse who needs to feel the weight of their choices. I also don't want to put more boundaries in place than is necessary. Help me to find the balance Lord and to trust your leadership. In Jesus Name. Amen.

Step #10

Choose Love

I was sprawled out on the floor begging God to take the pain away. I was also begging Him to show me what to do. Truth be told, I was demanding He tell me what to do. I was absolutely lost on how to handle this situation I had just discovered several weeks earlier. He had agreed to get help and was registered for the Every Man's Battle seminar in a few weeks. I had discovered he hadn't stopped talking to her so I just didn't know what to do.

"God, what do you want me to do?" I choked out in tears.

"I want you to love him," God whispered to my heart. It wasn't an audible voice but rather His truth that moved from my head to my heart.

"I don't know if you've noticed, but he's not real lovable right now," I defended.

"I don't know if you've noticed," He whispered back, "but sometimes you aren't either."

"Okay, God, you're right. You love me when I'm unlovable. You're going to have to show me how to do that."

Shortly after that, God took me to Romans 12:9-21. It became my guidebook for loving someone who wasn't loving me back. Here's an excerpt:

> Let love be genuine. Abhor what is evil; hold fast to what is good. Love one another with brotherly affection. Outdo one another in showing honor. Do not be slothful in zeal, be fervent in spirit, serve the Lord. Rejoice in hope, be patient in tribulation, be constant in prayer. Contribute to the needs of the saints and seek to show hospitality.
>
> Bless those who persecute you; bless and do not curse them. Rejoice with those who rejoice, weep with those who weep. Live in harmony with one another. Do not be haughty, but associate with the lowly. Never be wise in your own sight. Repay no one evil for evil, but give thought to do what is honorable in the sight of all. If possible, so far as it depends on you, live peaceably with all. Beloved, never avenge yourselves, but leave it to the wrath of God, for it is written, "Vengeance is mine, I will repay, says the Lord." To the contrary, if your enemy is hungry, feed him; if he is thirsty, give him something to drink; for by so doing you will heap burning coals on his head. Do not be overcome by evil, but overcome evil with good. (ESV)

Doing things God's way is often not easy but it's always right. It can also make an impression on others in powerful ways. Please know that I didn't do it perfectly and you won't either. There was one night after Mark left when the toilet overflowed on the 2nd floor and the water went all the way to the basement. I wasn't loving that night at all when I called him and gave him a piece of my mind. So I definitely still had my moments of losing it. But all in all, I was learning to slow down my responses and give love where I would have given a tongue-lashing in the past. I felt like God was leading me more often than I was doing things my way.

After I'd been practicing this type of love for over six months, my husband asked me in frustration one night, "How have you treated me so kindly when I've treated you so badly?" I quickly responded, "I don't know, Mark. It's unhumanable." He chuckled at the word and so did I. He said, "What does that even mean?" I responded that it meant it wasn't me...it was God working in me and through me.

Later after he returned home, I shared these verses in Romans with him. When I read verse 20, he said, "That's what you did! You heaped burning coals upon my head!" When I asked him how I did that he said, "You treated me better than I deserved to be treated."

Love is powerful. Unconditional love is even more powerful. When God is maturing us, perfecting us to be more like Him, it can have powerful results.

Yes, it was still love when I put boundaries in place. Why? It was HOW I communicated those boundaries in a loving manner that didn't reciprocate the anger being expressed to me. It wasn't easy, but it kept me in a good place spiritually and emotionally and it spoke volumes to my husband on the receiving end. Even if he hadn't responded to the love, I would have been able to continue my journey in life knowing I did what God asked me to do.

Truth for Today

"Love is patient and kind; love does not envy or boast; it is not arrogant or rude. It does not insist on its own way; it is not irritable or resentful; it does not rejoice at wrongdoing, but rejoices with the truth. Love bears all things, believes all things, hopes all things, endures all things."
I Corinthians 13:4-7, ESV

Lord I confess that it's easy to love someone who is loving you back. I don't know how to love someone who isn't loving me back. Show me how. Grow me to understand love in a deeper way than I've ever understood it before. Thank you for loving me first. Help me to accept that unconditional love so I can learn to give it to others—especially those who are hard to love right now. In Jesus Name. Amen.

Final Thoughts

I'm so sorry for the pain you're experiencing. I wish it could be taken away with the snap of a finger. It can't though. I had to walk it out and you will have to as well.

However, God often does His best work through the cracks in our lives. He turns our messes into His messages. That's what He did with my mess and that's what He'll do with yours if you'll let Him.

Your message doesn't have to be writing a book or standing on a stage telling your story. It may just be sitting across the table in a coffee shop with someone experiencing what you experienced months or years earlier. You see, one way God redeems the broken places in our lives is to allow us to bring empathy, wisdom, and encouragement to others walking a similar path.

You're in a difficult situation full of fear and pain. However, if you'll walk by faith in this difficult season, you'll find yourself experiencing an inner strength, hope, and confidence (that I like to call Godfidence).

It is then that you will truly be able to say, "It is not well with my circumstances, but it is well with my soul."

"You will keep in perfect peace those whose minds are steadfast, because they trust in you."
Isaiah 26:3, NIV

"For I know the plans I have for you," declares the LORD, "plans to prosper you and not to harm you, plans to give you hope and a future."
Jeremiah 29:11, NIV

When trust has been broken, it can be rebuilt.

When you're ready to start that process, let us help you walk through the **Rebuilding Trust Roadmap.**

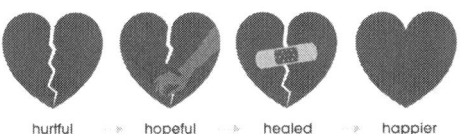

hurtful → hopeful → healed → happier

Appendix A

Mark and Jill Savage Resources

Blog: www.MarkandJill.org (You can subscribe to get encouragement in your inbox. Mark and I do Marriage Monday posts almost every Monday.)

No More Perfect Podcast: Find anywhere you listen to podcasts!

No More Perfect Marriages 10 Day Blog Series—this was a 10 day series Mark and I wrote together to share our story and give individuals and couples the help and hope they need. It's a valuable series for both healthy and hurting marriages. You can find it at www.markandjill.org/ourstory

Rebuilding Trust After An Affair: www.MarkandJill.org/affairrecovery

No More Perfect Marriages: Experience the Freedom of Being Real Together: this is our book that digs deep into the lessons learned in our crisis. Designed to help good marriages become great and hurting marriages find healing, *No More Perfect Marriages* will take your marriage to a deeper level of intimacy and freedom.

www.NoMorePerfectDateNight.com: This is a membership site we've created to strengthen marriages. Registration only opens in the Fall and Spring, but we are happy to allow those who purchase *Your Next Steps* the opportunity to join at any time. Simply email resources@jillsavage.org and we'll send you a link to get started.

No More Perfect Marriages Seminars: You can register for the next seminar (or join a wait list) at www.seminar.jillsavage.org. You can also inquire about bringing a seminar to your church or community at speaking@jillsavage.org.

No More Perfect Marriages eChallenge: This free four-week challenge can be a helpful resources for putting the broken pieces back together in a hurting marriage. Find at www.MarkandJill.org/marriagechallenge.

Marriage Coaching: Mark and I offer marriage coaching and marriage intensives. You can learn more at www.MarkandJill.org/marriagecoaching.

Appendix B

Bible Verses for Hard Times

Exodus 15:2 The Lord is my strength and my song; he has given me victory. This is my God, and I will praise him— my father's God, and I will exalt him!

Psalm 9:9-10 The Lord is a refuge for the oppressed, a stronghold in times of trouble.

Psalm 32:7-8 You are my hiding place; you will protect me from trouble and surround me with songs of deliverance.

Exodus 33:14 My presence will go with you, and I will give you rest.

Deuteronomy 31:8 It is the Lord who goes before you. He will be with you; he will not fail you or forsake you. Do not fear or be dismayed.

Deuteronomy 33:27 The eternal God is your refuge, and underneath are the everlasting arms.

Isaiah 30:15 In repentance and rest is your salvation, in quietness and trust is your strength.

Luke 12:25-26 Who of you by worrying can add a single hour to your life? Since you cannot do this very little thing, why do you worry about the rest?

Philippians 4:6 Do not worry about anything, but in everything by prayer and supplication with thanksgiving let your requests be made known to God. And the peace of God, which surpasses all understanding, will guard your hearts and your minds in Christ Jesus.

John 14:27 Peace I leave with you; my peace I give you. I do not give to you as the world gives. Do not let your hearts be troubled and do not be afraid.

Psalm 34:4 I sought the Lord, and he answered me, and delivered me from all my fears.

Psalm 27: 1-3 The LORD is my light and my salvation...whom shall I fear? The LORD is the stronghold of my life— of whom shall I be afraid? When the wicked advance against me to devour me, it is my enemies and my foes who will stumble and fall. Though an army besiege me, my heart will not fear; though war break out against me, even then I will be confident.

Joshua 1:9 Be strong and courageous; do not be frightened or dismayed, for the Lord your God is with you wherever you go.

Psalm 145: 18-19 The Lord is near to all who call on him, to all who call on him in truth. He fulfills the desires of those who fear him; he hears their cry and saves them.

1 Peter 5:7 Cast all your anxiety on him because he cares for you.

Isaiah 12:2 Surely God is my salvation; I will trust *and not be afraid*. The Lord, the Lord, is *my strength* and my song; he has become my salvation.

2 Timothy 1:7 For God did not give us a spirit of timidity, but a spirit of power, of love and of self-discipline.

Psalm 138:3 When I called, you answered me; you made me bold and stouthearted.

Psalm 16:8 I have set the Lord always before me. Because he is at my right hand, I will not be shaken.

Psalm 62:1-2 My soul finds rest in God alone; my salvation comes from him. He alone is my rock and my salvation; he is my fortress, I will never be shaken.

Psalm 91:1-2 You who live in the shelter of the Most High, who abide in the shadow of the Almighty, will say to the Lord, "My refuge and my fortress; my God in whom I trust."

2 Corinthians 12:9 My grace is sufficient for you, for my power is made perfect in weakness.

Philippians 4: 12-13 I know what it is to be in need, and I know what it is to have plenty. I have learned the secret of being content in any and every situation . . . I can do everything through him who gives me strength.

2 Thessalonians 3:3 But the Lord is faithful, and he will strengthen and protect you from the evil one.

Isaiah 40:29 He gives power to the weak and strength to the powerless.

1 Peter 5: 10 And the God of all grace, who called you to his eternal glory in Christ, after you have suffered a little while, will himself restore you and make you strong, firm and steadfast.

Hebrews 4:16 For we do not have a high priest who is unable to sympathize with our weaknesses, but we have one who in every respect has been tested as we are, yet without sin. Let us therefore approach the throne of grace with boldness, so that we may receive mercy and find grace to help in time of need.

Deuteronomy 31:6,8 Be strong and bold; have no fear or dread of them, because it is the Lord your God who goes before you. He will be with you; he will not fail you or forsake you. Do not fear or be dismayed.

2 Thessalonians 3:16 Now may the Lord of peace himself give you peace at all times and in every way.

Appendix C

Recommended Reading and Resources

Ready for more? Organized by topic, you may want to tap into some other resources Mark and I found helpful:

Healing from The Past
- *Not Marked: Finding Hope and Healing after Sexual Abuse* by Mary DeMuth
- *When The Man You Love Was Abused* by Cecil Murphy
- *Love Letters from the Edge: Meditations for Those Struggling with Brokenness, Trauma, and the Pain of Life* by Shelly Beach and Wanda Sanchez
- *Love Is a Choice: The Definitive Book on Letting Go of Unhealthy Relationships* by Frank Minirth and Paul Meier

Infidelity
- *Unfaithful: Hope and Healing After Infidelity* (this is a book Mark and I read aloud together after he came home.)
- Rebuilding Trust After an Affair - www.MarkandJill.org/affairrecovery
- *Healing Your Marriage When Trust Is Broken: Finding Forgiveness and Restoration* by Cindy Beall
- *Marriage Undercover: Thriving in a Culture of Quiet Desperation* by Bob and Audrey Meisner
- Every Man's Battle workshop – The Every Man's Battle Workshop is the place where men engage in the battle to get back their sexual integrity. *(Mark attended this and found it very helpful)*

- **Women in the Battle** workshop — Women in the Battle is designed to help women who have been hurt in relationships with men who are or have been involved in pornography, sexual addiction or adultery.

Marriage Books

(There are hundreds of wonderful marriage books out there. These three have had the most impact on us.)

- *No More Perfect Marriages: Experience the Freedom of Being Real Together*: this is our book that digs deep into the lessons learned in our crisis. Designed to help good marriages become great and hurting marriages find healing, *No More Perfect Marriages* will take your marriage to a deeper level of intimacy and freedom.
- *How We Love: Discover Your Love Style, Enhance Your Marriage* by Milan and Kay Yerkovich (This book is a MUST for any married couple. It absolutely transformed our relationship! We chose to read it aloud together. It took us months, but was worth every minute!)
- *The God Empowered Wife: How Strong Women Can Help Their Husbands Become Godly Leaders* (A Must-Read for wives!)

Marriage Events

- No More Perfect Marriages Conferences (Mark and I lead these events) - www.seminar.jillsavage.org
- Family Life "Weekend to Remember" Marriage Conferences

Midlife Crisis

- Midlife.com

- *Death of a Hero, Birth of the Soul: Answering the Call of Midlife* by John Robinson
- *Men in Midlife Crisis* by Jim Conway
- *Your Husband's Midlife Crisis* by Sally Conway

Music

- Cheri Keaggy's album *So I Can Tell* — This was powerful music for me during the painful season. Cheri wrote the music on this album after her husband left. It's beautiful, honest music culled out of a dark season of life.

Pain

- *Hearing Jesus Speak into Your Sorrow* by Nancy Guthrie
- *When the Hurt Runs Deep: Healing and Hope for Life's Desperate Moments* by Kay Arthur

Pornography

- *Every Man's Battle: Winning the War on Sexual Temptation One Victory at a Time (The Every Man Series)* by Stephen Arterburn
- *When Your Husband Is Addicted to Pornography: Healing Your Wounded Heart* by Vicki Tiede
- **Every Man's Battle** workshop– The Every Man's Battle Workshop is the place where men engage in the battle to get back their sexual integrity. *(Mark attended this and found it very helpful)*
- **Women in the Battle** workshop — Women in the Battle is designed to help women who have been hurt in relationships with men who are or have been involved in pornography, sexual addiction or adultery.

Protecting Your Marriage
- *Close Calls: What Adulterers Want You to Know About Protecting Your Marriage* by Dave Carder

Separation and Divorce
- *Broken Heart on Hold: Surviving Separation* by Linda Rooks
- *When He Leaves: Help and Hope for Hurting Wives* by Kari West and Noelle Quinn
- *When Your Marriage Dies* by Laura Petherbridge

Spiritual Renewal
- Holy Bible– I personally love the ESV version and The Message version on occasion.
- *The God Who Sees You: Look to Him When You Feel Discouraged, Forgotten, or Invisible* by Tammy Maltby
- *Never Ever Be the Same: A New You Starts Today* by Larry and Kathy Miller

Dear Reader,

I'd love to hear how this book encouraged you personally! You can email me at jill@jillsavage.org. You can also find me on:

    Facebook: www.facebook.com/jillsavage.author

    Instagram: @jillsavage.author

    Twitter: @jillsavage

You'll also find more encouragement at my blog and website: www.jillsavage.org.

Joining you in the journey,

Jill

Made in the USA
Monee, IL
05 September 2021